Tales of a Mystic's Journey

Wisdom Flows From the Heart Not the Mind

By: Piro Papa

This collection of poetry put simply, is Sharing a Heart
of an awakened one.

Printed in the United States of America

DeeJak's
PUBLISHING COMPANY

DeeJak's Publishing Company
7209- J East W.T. Harris Blvd # 279
Charlotte, NC 28227-1004
980-272-1166
www.deejakspublishing.com

Cover and layout design by: Crystal Jeffrey
ISBN: 978-0-9857903-7-0
Library of Congress Control Number: 2015952079

Table of Contents

Preface

More often than not, our experiences and perceptions of reality fall within a slim and constricted margin of understanding and possibilities. We constantly see ourselves with a critical gaze; focusing on our flaws, hindrances, and desires forever out of our reach. What then, does a world free of such limiting convictions look like and more importantly, how do we access it? This collection of poetry, written by someone much like yourself, who has experienced wearing such self-imposed shackles and HAS attained sweet liberation from them, will provide you with a glimpse of the light of understanding that will allow you to unbind your body, mind, and spirit. Through these conversations with the self, you will discover from discussions of mind and thought, heart and love, and the breaking of boundaries; THAT you yourself will be able to see the true meaning of liberation and unconditional love and experience yourself far beyond this imprisoning physical reality; traveling far into the infinity of bliss and serenity.

Piro shows us that if we can open up our hearts and expand our minds then we can bring them into synchronicity. It is then that we will no longer be bound by limitations and we too can achieve spiritual growth and align ourselves with the flow of the universe. Once we start to flow with the universe instead of against it... things that were once impossible.... Now become possible...

1

Truth

Is like a sail ship
named Peace
blown forward by the wind
of love in the infinite sea
of tranquility

2

My Heart Sees

It's a whisper in the air
an ancient wisdom for us to prepare.
The sacred heart sharing with the mind
Brother surrender in me
That will set you free

You have been a prisoner of your temporary world
while I have been your infinite existence all along
you are the forever conquering wave
you are the creation of emotions
the painter of colors
the seeker of imagination
try surrendering in me
I have loving feelings for you to color and see

I am the stillness and peace
the depth of your sea
I will give you the wings to fly into yourself and into me
and I will open your inner eyes to see the magnificence of eternity
the truth which is in you and what surrenders us

I will show you the true nature of the only reality
which is love below and above
surrender, surrender to me!
set yourself free

3

Spirit Inquiry

Who am I
Why am I here?
So many keys
so many doors to fear
The more I know the more I find
My ears are deaf
My eyes are blind
In the day
I build my sense
In the night dreams
I change my mind
Who am I?
What do I know?
Why in the day
Life seems to be
a bit slow
but in the night
I am not here
No anguish

No limits
And the pain of fear

Nowhere near
Just the vast emptiness
And the voice of love
Whispering to me
You belong here
In the dream
I have no "why"
In the dream
Ohhhhhhh, I truly fly
And the happiness becomes earth and sky
In my heart
I do know that life and death
Are here to show
That there is nothing to grieve
Nothing to leave
Awareness and life
beams of light for us to weave
That is why
My friends
I always say
To remember
Love and light
That is why
We are here

4

The Consciousness is You

You know it will be untrue
You know it will be a lie
If someone tells to you
That you cannot get any higher
So come on and light your fire

The consciousness is You
The inner mirror knows no liar
This world can do nothing to you
let the storm of life blow into your fire
It will never put it out
But make it grow wider and higher
So come on and light your fire

This always has been with you
This always has been your only desire
For the time to come
The awareness in you to set your heart on fire
Come on, come on, come on
The consciousness is you

5

The Monk and the Light

Light know the language of the silent monk
Always calling him near
Look at me there is no distinction where I shine
Hug like me
Kiss like me
Embrace earth
Embrace sky
Embrace life
Embark on your journey without "why"
You are created to be free
To live in harmony
So that is why you do not have to pick and choose
You want to be like me;
To have nothing to lose
Let me shine in your heart
That is as heavy as a cast
And that hard rock of pain will turn to dust
Open your heart for me
I will change it to a beautiful flower
For everyone to smell and see

Let us unify in unconditional love

That is in your heart
And you will become the monk that carries the light

6

Silent and Alone

Often people ask me
"Where did you go? You are not here.
You are silent and alone."
I have no words to explain where I have gone
My place and my view
They can be in my place and have my view
Or better, have their own
Only if they become
Silent and alone

7

Destiny and Freewill

Destiny and freewill are like two sides of a coin
Holding it in our hand
When we see one side we are holding the other
Our destiny is to have freewill
As our creator intended
When we reach that
It will be unity
No more destiny or freewill
Just eternity

8

What I See

God is everywhere
It is not a captive of Heaven
What creates Heaven and Hell?
Is our mind's inability to accept infinity
There is no rest in creation
There is no final destination
It is an amazing love communication
That will always bring us beyond what we know and experience
in this form and beyond

Don't make Heaven a place of yours to be,
Bring it here on Earth
For other beings to experience and see

We are all passing through
Like the wind with no destination
Bringing to this Earth
Frequencies of our vibration
And that wind is you
The non-form, the mystical wind of renown

Flying through universes and galaxies
That's what you are and that's what I see

9

Aware

Becoming aware of how the temporary form
and experience affects the permanent
Infinite and formless to change
It's a mesmerizing mystery of God
Changes of vibrations are embodied to our essence
And will constitute your next experience
This is the proof for eternity
Changes after changes
And experiences through infinity
It is the spirit evolution with out destiny
In this creation there is no limitation
There is no destination
Only you and the creation
With infinite combinations

Knowing this is what will set you free
No more dogmas and religions
What you have received up until now
It will be ignorance when tomorrow comes
With new inspirations about the creation

And with this we move on and on
Realizing we belong to this awesome infinite creation

You Are

Do not look up to God
For love or favors or answers
It has nothing more because it gave all to you
What it has you have
Love, power, intelligence, wisdom
Find it in yourself and use it
You have the power to create as you are
When you move the creation moves
When you think the creation thinks
Your inspiration triggers God's imagination
It is an equal determination for the continuance of creation

God's creativity is like the wind and the sea
The one without the other cannot be
As the wind blows over the sea and creates waves
God blows in you the breath of creation and bring deep
inspirations in your heart
And waves of thought in your mind
As inspirations create imaginations
They reflect on this Earth and beyond
In ways that you never thought possible

That you can reach so far
With an open heart
You know limitation cannot be
Love is the only ingredient in the creation
Love will make you see what stands between you and God
Which is a sleeping mind that you call "me"
Where you always have been the "I"
The nameless, the formless, the God consciousness

Knowing

Knowing who you are
Why you are here
Who put you on the Earth?
Who arranged your time here?
With expansion of awareness
you can look back at your life
And consciously understand your existence
that eliminates judgment

Experiencing life here on Earth
Is a tough class
With all of the pain and struggling
For surviving it's hard to have
Peace in the mind
But there is a message hidden in this realm!
That's what we need
for our awareness to become more keen
to see the temporary reality
of the form and the pain and fear we live
it is not from within .

We are all connected
but at the same time we are on our own
changing your vibrations will send unique waves
through all connections
So what, if the world will judge?
We all have different minds
But still can find harmony
As different notes in a beautiful symphony

Reborn

I have been surrounded by you
I have been breathing you
You have carried me
As the mother carries the baby in her belly
I have been blind but now
I see your love has always surrounded me
And always will
Like the mother who loves her child in the belly
The same as when it is born

You loved me the same when I was blind and ignorant
And now that I see
I am happy I feel your love
I can hug and kiss you
Although my words are limited
You understand me to the deepest feelings
Because I speak your language now of silence and tranquility

I have the most beautiful laughter
And the loudest too

But then again,
Only you can hear it
What is this love?
My mind cannot describe it
But my heart knows it
All the love I have for you
My heart and my existence is yours
O God of marvelousness and miracle
Sustainer of creation

Waking Up

How strange it is
How beautiful it is
To know and acknowledge
The continuation of life beyond this reality
It is freedom knowing myself
As an existence out of this earth
And at the same time I am connected to the life on Earth
To every living source
I am experiencing humbleness, compassion, sympathy,
and humility here
Everyone that I interact with is my teacher and all virtues
are becoming wings of my spirit
I am flying in the infinite awareness
I am becoming aware of the unconditional love that serves me
And I understand that I am a mirror reflecting, reflecting
The unconditional love in and around me

Selfless

Memories of the past
Achievement and position
Successes and failures
What constitutes you?
Let it go, let it go
It is the fog that has surrounded you
It is the veil of your inner eyes
The path to awareness is selfless
To walk the selfless path is to surrender to the formless
To surrender to the mystery
Then you will become the peace itself
Your actions will be made in tranquility
When you are selfless you hold nothing
But you love everything
Only then the knowing starts to flow
Only then you will see that forms come and go
But your essence will always remain to play
With the infinite ocean of existence you are timeless
boundless the love itself
Selfless, you will become the ever-loving fountain of love
That time cannot touch
And all of your brothers and sisters will rest in you

And be nourished by your flowing love
Let go your thoughts of ambitions
You are made to hold nothing
But you are made to love everyone and everything

Awakening

I fall asleep and dream again
In a moonless night
The mystery of what is beyond the stars came to my mind
And then you came and moved the stars away
It was like the curtains of a show opening
And I was in love instantly with the light
That exists beyond the curtains dressed with stars
I could not speak
Love had surrounded me
Silence became my language
And I knew that this conversation and expression of feelings will
last for infinity
As the love I have for you
I see no distance between you and I
I am no longer a spectator
I passed the curtains
I am a part of your love
I am a part of your existence
You are my father
You are my mother
And a child of yours I will always be

My Inner Cry

Lament, oh lament
As long as I remember my life
I had myself in front of me and I had endless needs
Unconquered desires
Until you came into my unaware life
O God of love and endless existence
You came in front of me with no form
Silence and tranquility was your presence
I surrender myself to you
And I was surrendered by your love
At that moment I knew that surrendering to you
Was what my heart was longing for
I have never had such a sweet lament for you and your love
Oh what a feeling to know that my heart has been longing
for so long
To know that the thirst of the heart is quenched by the love
of God is freedom
Now that I know you
I know the purpose of my existence
I have no needs,
I have loveI am in love with you

God my sustainer
The creator of love
The creator of life
Lament, lament
Oh what happiness to live in your love

Vibrations

Vibration is everything
It is the creation
The form you are living and the imagination have no differences
Those exist because of vibrations
Creation is an infinite mirror of vibrations
And your frequency constitutes your reality
Waking up to this truth
One word comes in the heart
Responsibility
Do not let your vibrations be affected by violence and greed
This is the message of the creation indeed
Look at the life around you
Selfish existence based on manipulation, greed, and deception
There is no responsibility out of those vibrations
Love, sympathy, compassion
It is the awakened ONE reality
Where responsibility becomes a sacred word for eternity

Wisdom is to Surrender

Surrender, surrender
To the wisdom of the heart
It is there in your heart where love exists, not in your mind
Heart know no right or wrong
Heart does not know the words "I belong"
It is a temple of love where your inner being is always free
It is there where you merge with infinity
It is in your heart to find love and when you truly see
Only from your heart you can love your mind
You can show it that there is nothing to gain, nothing to lose,
nothing to seek, nothing to find
Always surrounded by love, in front and behind
Surrender, surrender to the wisdom of your heart
It will set you free in a place where there is no you and
there is no me
Just infinite love where feelings of the heart say, "just be"

Find Your Own Way

As a caravan that lost it's way in the desert
We are following each other with the fear
That the oasis is nowhere near
Until an old man dares to speak
No one was paying attention to him
He was old and he was weak
Follow the sun, follow the sun
It will guide us there
His light the point of reference
This guidance has been given to us all along
And we ignore it because we have a group where we belong
A caravan of its own
The light of wisdom is in front of him, the leader
As it is in front of you
With no preferences as the sun to all of the people--
of the caravan
There is no leader following the light
We all have that right
Lift the veils of your eyes
And see God's light
And confidence will always be in your sight

Lead yourself to awareness
No one will walk your path for you
Embrace yourself in this earthly experience
And know that freedom is love and love is light

No Inquiry (A Lesson from the Ceremony)

In my deepest vision again
I saw my relation to the creation
It has no path
It walks not in a journey
But it blooms like a thousand-petal rose, constant and firm
In all directions
I see myself as a quiet pond reflecting the sky of creation
And my awareness in the middle
Looking at the sky above and the sky below
Reflected in the water
Only in peace I know the creation
The deeper the peace the deeper the reflection
I feel excited
I want to talk about it
Then immediately I know if I will do so
I'll create waves of disturbance
And I will lose that perfect reflection
So I let it be
The tranquil reflection of creation
Is the peace in me?
that is the infinite blooming rose of eternity
With roots in tranquility

The Words are Short of....

Truth is when you just be
Not what you know
Truth is a state of being
Not of knowing or seeing
Trying to explain it brings only complications
In synchronicity with truth
You forget what you are
You forget what you have become
It is just you
The light surrounded by love below and above
Being the truth
You have nothing to solve
It is relaxing, replenishing
It is deep peace to be in the state of no thought
Where there is nothing to remember
Or worry that you forgot
All of the knowing and the thoughts of the past
Have been your mirror's dust
Shaking that dust
Letting it fall free

It will make the surface of the mirror
shiny and clean
Mirroring the pure awareness as it comes in
And that is just the beginning!

Changing Reality

Children of the sky
Remember you came in this reality without a "why"
Transformed in this human form you forgot your infinity
All of your thoughts are for this form
And on this Earth you have convinced yourself that it is here
where you belong
Here with all the beautiful colors
With sounds and songs
Human relations with joy and fear and sorrows
You ignore your infinity
You touch, smell, hear, see, and say
That this is reality and not some imaginary spirit of infinity
What is this infinity?
What good will it do in this life for me?
Should I leave all of those experiences for something?
I do not feel and see?
Having these thoughts you got stuck in this reality
You forgot the continuity
You forgot that you came from eternity
And after this experience

Life will still be in existence
This is not the first time you are experiencing a form
And on this planet is not where you belong
It is only a temporary act to perform
Seeing feeling the continuity of life will change this reality
You will not be selfish looking for joy, riches, knowledge,
and comfort
Only for yourself
Instead you will share it and spread
Acknowledging your spirit and continuity in infinity
It will turn you into a universal bee
Going from reality to reality spreading the seeds of love
and harmony

The Mystery of Aya (A Wonder of the Ceremony)

Mother Aya who is sure that all that glitters is love and honesty
Is showing me my way to life in eternity
There are a lot of thoughts in me and she wants me to make
sure they have love and honesty
And they are not another mind fantasy
As I start wondering to get the true meaning
I see my body and I feel that the spirit is crying for leaving
But she says, "Not from your body you are not leaving.
You need it for care and love-giving."
And as I speak into my mind
Is that the truth? Is that worth living?
And she says "Yes, if you want to progress. You stay with your
body if you love yourself and if you love me."
And in my heart and in my mind I see the bright light shine
in front of my face
And all I feel is an amazing grace

Mind

What a beautiful creation is the mind
Make apparent and dissolves realities
It shines breathless formations
And paints awesome imaginations
But for the wise ones
Those who can see
What sustains the mind?
They see its roots come from the heart
From the heart mind takes the inspiration
To create colors, vibrations, and love relations
Without the heart mind cannot speak
Without the heart mind cannot sing
Heart is the conductor
Mind the orchestra
And both play the composed spirit symphony
The mysterious music of eternity
Mind without the heart in existence cannot be
And heart without the mind cannot make love shine
With this wisdom our existence
Becomes balanced

With an open heart life thrives

With an open mind life shines
They are both wings of the spirit
Carry it; flying through infinity

In Silence

Be silent and listen to the messages of creation
They will reveal to you the true identity
The meaning of what is "I" and what is "Me"
What is spirit and what is form?
In silence you are on your own
It is in silence when God transcends
And takes you far along and with love
It will show what you are and where you came from
Only in silence you will understand
How it is not to have a name and form
In silence you embrace your intuition
And see that God is love through eternity
Any name, any form for it
Has been your imagination feeding from this reality
The most honest conversation is held in silence
With humbleness and sincerity
In silence you accept you divinity
Those are virtues that will open your inner sight
To see and feel the true light
In silence you learn your relative existence in the creation

Only in silence you have that revelation
In silence you always will return to connect with eternity
Where unconditional love becomes you
Where God has no name, no form--
where mysteries of renown are shown

Forgiveness or Acceptance

Forgiveness it is an expression of the spirit
Experiencing a human form
With forgiveness we create nobility of our own
But will forgiveness exist without humility?
So who has the nobility and who has the humility?
The one who asks or the one who gives?
Both I will say if you ask me
But this is not the reality
He who gives forgiveness wants the nobility
And he who asks for forgiveness always gets the humility
Looking in ourselves we will solve this controversy in my heart
I see that there is no such thing as forgiving others or myself
I see, feel nothing but acceptance of what they or I have been
In a temporary ignorance for a time seeing
In acceptance I see no judgment
I see awareness, in different speed of acceleration
That creates uniqueness but not separation
I accept my actions with all of the flaws and the awes
As forgiveness bring nobility
Acceptance bring humbleness for me

Acceptance is a virtue of eternity
And with this in mind I know it will continue
beyond this reality

Observing

Being conscious of your direct line with the form
And observing it with no distractions
From any reality that you are in
Is to be the observer
When observing your life wisdom becomes apparent
It is at that moment that you feel the "I"
It is at that moment that you know what adolescence is
And what it means to grow
That maturity is awareness in spirit
Not because of the appearance or age of your form
Observing my actions and thoughts of the past
I can see the changes that happened to me
These are like letters that I had written
And as I revisit them
They don't mean the same
It is difficult to be an observer
To pull yourself from the actions of this life
But if you will not do it
Life will do it for you
Imagine yourself as an old man

Quitting life's crazy run
Desperately saying,
"I am tired. Truly, I am finished. I am done.
But what a surprise, just when you thought life pushed
you aside, invisible, alone."
No one to see, no one to visit, you find yourself sitting
in the front seat
In your invisibility and peace you see everyone's speeds
and feel everyone's heartbeats
While they struggle writing the letters of their own lives
And a beautiful smile comes to your face
Because you know that all of those written life letters
Will have a beautiful reverse
And you will call it God's grace
With the life but not within it
It is when observing becomes keen
Only then you can be aware of progress that
for so long was unseen
In observing you are not passive or weak
You have just passed this material life, flashy and greed
And inside of you observing infinitely
You know this is the only reality

Reality the Me

Mirrors of vibrations everywhere
Showing my form the performance of me
Struggling with and loving this temporary reality
Since my birth all my thoughts were generated around this form
That this shape is called Human and Earth is the only home
And the people around me taught the ranks in society and
history as inspiration for me
That wars are so important for the evolution of humanity
"Hmm." They speak of Alexander; he went to fight beyond the
Mediterranean Sea to conquer the world
Because of his fighting and conquering almost the entire world
they call him "Alexander the Great."
They speak to me about Hitler--
he did the same, but they didn't call him the "great."
Instead they call him the "dictator" and the "bad"
"Hmm." And they say that the world is finally free
or almost
except for a few wars that are going to help spread
freedom and democracy
confused from history
lets grab and read some biology
where making me believe that there is a monkey's gene in me

that spirit does not exist
that reality is what we can touch and hold on smell or see, at
least and my lineage springs out of a beast
"Hmm."
All of the his-stories and bio-logies are here to make me
express my interpretation
And my story and to set myself free
So at this moment the human form that is me,
is apparently temporary
As is this reality
And the I becomes present as the only infinite existence
beyond human form
And earth as a home setting myself free no more a prisoner
of his-story or bio-logy
Theology and on
I know it is up to my desire
What to learn and what to inquire
I have different eyes to see this temporary reality
It is an important class to learn how to break my mental jar glass
And consciously remember that our roots are divine

No matter in what temporary reality we are in
We are made to shine
That life experiences are to be experienced and left behind
As spirit we will move on
Not turning back

To this reality
Creation knows no repetition
This is freedom's fruition

29

Universal Mother

So much to say for my sacred mother
For the divine feminine that gives me love and grace
And from all of the names I love to call her Space
In her is where I grow
In her is where I build the know
And I am mesmerized by the love that she can show
With her teachings and care
I know she is the only universal Mother with no compare
She is in me and around me
Feeding unending love-energy vibration
Awakening in me the infinity of creation
She always is showing me that changing thoughts means
changing forms
That is how creations works, moves, and performs
Acting from inspiration is always in rejuvenation
And space expanding to infinity is a never-ending continuation
of awareness in me
By her showing me the continuity
I have become aware of immortality
She opened my inner eyes to see eternity

And how to free myself from my ignorant perception of demise
That death is true and I could not see without physical eyes
Through her love I have grown
I have recognized I have a space of my own
By expanding that I see myself mature
And always moving towards the unknown
With no fear for the new reality
Convinced that it will still be love with a new frequency
Love is endless and will always trigger transformation
With this in mind I close my eyes
In silence and experience the Sacred Mother's brilliance
I see her eyes that peer deep into my being
There is nothing about her that is unseeing
Nothing that I can hide or make wrong look right
It is incredible, her intelligence
Nothing escapes from her
Not even a glace
Looking her in the eyes
I accept the right and the wrong
The weakness and the strong in me
And she says "This is honesty"
That honest first, I must become
Before I ask the world why they don't have it
And what is wrong

When I spoke all of my deeds
Shared the deepest secrets
Emptied myself of pride
And false ego slime
I felt weak and waited to be judged
To my surprise no judgment came from her
Only love and care
And I was able to see when I am as empty as I can be
Without pride or thoughts to hold on
That's where I am the most strong
I always remember the Sacred Mother's advice
That only love will open my inner eyes
That love is the holistic connection between you and me
the only permanent reality in the creation

Light and Intelligence

Light is intelligence
That has acknowledged its presence with no interference
There would be no light if intelligence were not searching
The continuation of creation is based upon light and
intelligence progression
There are infinite beautiful forms in the creation
All of those inspiring shapes and colors
Cannot share messages if light did not shine
Not only does light make form visible
But in ourselves has the power to transform
It is amazing awareness to know the ability of light
To see how light works in this temporary reality
And how this always has been the foundation of eternity
As intelligence directs light
Light nourish intelligence
From that always comes the ability to see
The same hindrance not to be a prisoner of any
temporary reality
But to be conscious of our internal essence
That is what I call universal presence
Time is temporary

It is an ingredient that makes every experience extraordinary
Acknowledging this is what enlightens intelligence
And always remembers its presence
That light is its own circumference
The more intelligence grows the more light shows
Intelligence is the ether, the unseen
Where light is the particle and the mass
Intelligence thinks and light makes it appear
When intelligence and light are aligned
It becomes obvious that nothing is hidden
It is a mystery expanding into the mystery
Intelligence the right and light the left foot of spirit
Taking steps into eternity
Reality after reality
And forever like this it will be

31

Walking and Flying

Flying is what we all do
Walking is what we come here to experience and dance to
Our feet are like the hands of a clock
Moving step-by-step
Towards experiences that await
Feet don't just move mechanically
They are directed by thoughts
Walking with our feet we are walking with our thoughts
A step, a thought
Passing through every life station
And not being aware that with every new step
Every new thought
We leave every old one behind
With only memories to remind
We cannot recall the old steps
Only people, places, and events
Those who gave us a chill
And those who make us dance and thrilled
With those memories as a milestone
Walking and dancing and climbing the mountains

Stepping through forest and cities
What a blessing we are experiencing
All of this because of our form
Hugging and kissing each other
But then again we are alone
Leading ourselves to unique experiences of our own
Though all of those experiences every walk makes time
in its own
And at a moment of stagnation
A flashpoint of limitation comes to mind
With all of the places that we visit and leave behind
And with all of the wants that we have in mind
We still feel the limitations of this reality
And flying clearly becomes the only freedom's remedy
It all starts as inspiration from the heart you see
A yearning for a total freedom
From a source beyond this form
It has the power to free its own
In the beginning it flies out of the form
And then over the trees
It looks like a little bird that makes its virgin flight
And then empowers itself to roam the skies
Then inspiration takes higher acceleration
And flies to the moon and the sun
And why not, take the other planets into consideration

And then focuses on the stars
It wants to visit them all
One by one, every constellation
They seem to it jewels of its own creation
And at that moment
BAM!
An awesome intelligence explosion
A deeper awareness comes to place
That this reality is infinite self-interpretation
Walking or flying in this reality
With all of the planets and the stars
All of the beautiful galaxies
It still sees limitation
At that moment the infinite essence knows itself
That exists beyond any manifestation
That it was created free beyond any reality
And always will be
Walking or flying
Laughing or crying
Are all temporary experiences that expand our awareness?
To remember its essence
And not to forget it because of the form
What reality then will be?

You and me remembering our infinity
And sharing it through this reality

Limitation will dissolve like salt in the sea
Whom to call father mother brother or daughter
Those names and relations are based on a temporary reality
Isn't it beautiful?
That awareness of infinity
To share this life experience without the false ego of "me"
to see the infinite I that connects with everything
by not asking: WHY;

32

The Key to the Mystery

So many teachings
So many songs
Prayers and poems
Have been written to the mystery
Some call it God
Some call it eternity
The wonders in the teachings
The love in the songs
The hope in the prayers
The inspirations in the poems
All are sparked by the mystery of God in us
Without identity

Open your inner eyes
And see how many people
Fore eons have kneeled
Passionately learning from their teachers the meaning
of this life
And what reality means
Open your inner ears and listen to the songs again
How many people sing and dance

Laugh and cry
For something that is beyond they're fleshy ears and eyes
But through those songs and dances
They have transcended before their eyes
To something priceless
Pure self
That can never be compromised
Open your inner heart and listen to the prayers
It will have a deeper meaning
You will see spirits climbing towards the light
And prayers as the flame of courage
to embrace the path that looks tough and hard
you will hear them saying that love is the only way to eternity
and prayers are love's remedy
open your imagination
let it fly away
like a space rocket
fueled by mystery's inspiration
and as you visit new places where no one has gone
take a pen and write those experiences in a poem
tell me what you see
as you travel far and beyond this reality
then write what you feel
write what you think
of you and what you think of me
maybe you will see what I have seen

that each one of us is the key to the mystery
we are hearing this message
this ancient echo
going on and on
generation after generation in humanity
passed on through teachings, prayers, poems, and songs
so embark on your inner journey
fly yourself though the mysteries of eternity
and bring your knowledge here to awake humanity
be part of the Earth's sacred history

33

Fear no Fear

In my journey again
I awake from a long dream
My eyes were in pain from shedding tears
My body was shaking like a little flower that stands
on the cliff above the ocean
Constantly moved by the wind
I was crying upon my memories for a vibrational
state of existence
Where there is no pain
I was crying for this heavy load of form
That I am bearing
I was crying for all humanity
Without any thought of what they are doing
And what they should be
Just crying and crying
Knowing that they are carrying the same load as me
As my body shook rhythmically
I noticed it was because the tremendous love I was taking
All of that energy
It was making me able to see all of those things
To see God in everything

To understand why it is unseen
One of my tears transformed into a huge ball
And called me to come near
As I approached my memory started getting clearer
And in that ball of tear
I saw all of my countless journeys in God's creation
All of my spirit to form transformation
In all of them I heard one phrase
No fear, I'm always here
That was so amazing
All that information
Billions and billions of form's transformations
In a drop of tear
In that tear I saw the possibility of manifestation
in all of creation
I saw love everywhere I could go
I saw love in what I thought was the lowest of the low
And I saw love when I thought to go as high as I can go
Mesmerized by the possibilities in my drop of tear
I saw love's abilities to heal
So I touched it and it was real
And I decided to walk in it and disappear
Into my own drop of tear
Saying loud,
"Do not fear the fear!

34

God the Unseen

God the Creator
It is unseen
The sustainer of existence
The sustainer of creation
Exist only as an infinite frequency vibration
Seeing God in a form
Will be limitation
God is infinite energy vibration
Beyond any tangible or mental imagination
Synchronizing your spirit's vibration with it in harmony
Is the only true manifestation?
The higher spirit frequency
The deeper the conversation
With the intangible God of creation
In our heart we create vibrations
Only in our heart we create the proclamation
Of what we are
And from our heart we hold the conversation
With God of creation
Not from form to form

Not from being to being
But from unseen to unseen
With the language of love
The most sublime of all ways of communication
Which is the only connection in the creation
God is love and love is real
With this in our heart
We will keep our mind keen
To cut through any temporary form
Created by any reality
Talking with God but not with an entity
Only with undefined vibrations of eternity

35

Where Atoms Disappear

Life and death is appearance and disappearance of form
Appearance and disappearance is a fundamental principle
of creation
It is this action that keeps the creation moving
It is this action that keeps the creation always in rejuvenation
So where do atoms goes when they disappear
In a new probability to experience a new possibility
It is showing us our infinity
Although the disappearance is happening in silence
The message is loud and clear
Death is the beginning of a new probability
Death of the form is for the spirit to move on n another world,
death means continuity

36

Convinced

If seeing is believing
Feeling is knowing

LOVE and LIGHT

www.ingramcontent.com/pod-product-compliance
Lightning Source LLC
Chambersburg PA
CBHW020518030426
42337CB00011B/448

* 9 7 8 0 9 8 5 7 9 0 3 7 0 *